INTERNATIONAL DICTIONARY
OF
OBSCENITIES

A GUIDE TO
DIRTY WORDS
AND
INDECENT EXPRESSIONS
IN

SPANISH

ITALIAN

FRENCH

GERMAN

RUSSIAN

by

Christina Kunitskaya-Peterson

SCYTHIAN BOOKS

PRINTED IN U.S.A.

ISBN 0-933884-18-4

CONTENTS

USE OF DICTIONARY

English has no exact stylistic equivalent for some words and phrases in the other languages. For example, залупа, 'glans penis', a very vulgar and frequently encountered word in Russian, has no widely known counterpart in English. Thus, the author has sometimes used a relatively innocuous, neutral English word or phrase to translate what might be considered an unimaginable horror by some speakers of the other language.

Whenever possible, idiomatic translations of the words and phrases have been supplied. In cases where the literal meaning is obscured as a result, it is provided in brackets. Since many of the entries could be translated by any of several American English synonyms, a relatively small number of words are used repeatedly in the translations, while a much larger selection of them may be found in the final chapter, arranged under generic headings.

English	German	Russian
anus	ass(-hole)	Arsch(loch)	жопа, (очко)
break wind, to	to fart	furzen	пердеть, бздеть
breasts	tits	Titten	титьки
buttocks	ass	Arsch	жопа
condom	rubber	Gummi, Pariser	гондон, нахуйник
copulate, to	to fuck	vögeln, ficken	ебать
defecate, to	to shit	scheißen	срать
diarrhea	runny shits	Dünnschiß	(дрист)
erection	hard on	Ständer	
erection, to have an	to have a hard on	einen Ständer haben	стоять *у кого*
feces	shit	Scheiße	говно
fellate, to	to blow	blasen	отсосать, делать минет
fellatio	blow job		отсос, минет
homosexual	fag	Schwule	жоп(оч)ник
intestinal gas	fart	Furz	(бздо)
masturbate, to	to jack off, beat off	wichsen	дрочить
orgasm, to have	to come	kommen	кончить
penis	prick, cock	Schwanz	хуй
prostitute	whore	Hure	блядь
semen	come, jissom		малафья
testicles	balls	Eier	яйца, муди
toilet	can, john	Scheißhaus, Pißort	нужник, сортир
urinate, to	to piss	pissen	сцать
urine	piss	Piss(e)	сцаки
vagina	cunt	Fotze	пизда

Spanish	Italian	French	
(ojo del) culo	culo	(trou du) cul	anus
peerse, pederse	scoreggiare	péter	break wind, to
tetas	tette	nichons	breasts
culo	culo, (chiappe)	cul	buttocks
goma	guanto	capote anglaise	condom
joder, coger	fottere, fregare	baiser	copulate, to
cagar	cacare	chier	defecate, to
cagalera	cacarella	chiasse	diarrhea
	cazzo duro	bandaison	erection
pararse, empalmarse	rizzarsi, avere il cazzo duro	bander	erection, to have an
mierda, cagada	merda, cacca	merde	feces
mamar	fare un bocchino / pompino	prendre la pipe, sucer	fellate, to
mamada	bocchino, pompino	plume, pipe	fellatio
maricón	finocchio	enculé, pédale, enculeur	homosexual
pedo	peto, scoreggia	pet	intestinal gas
hacer puñetas, hacerse una paja	farsi una sega / pipa	se branler	masturbate, to
correrse	venire	jouir	orgasm, to have
carajo, pija, picha	cazzo	bite, queue	penis
puta	puttana	putain	prostitute
leche	sburro	jus, foutre	semen
cojones	coglioni	couilles, couillons	testicles
cagadero, meadero	cacatoio, pisciatoio	pissoir, pissotière	toilet
mear	pisciare	pisser	urinate, to
meados	piscia	pisse	urine
coño	fica, fregna, mona	con	vagina

SPANISH

almeja *f.* twat, vagina ['clam']

amaricado 1. *m.* fag, homosexual 2. *adj.* effeminate

amaricarse to become a fag/homosexual [*from* maricón 'homosexual']

argolla *f.* box, vagina ['ring; door-knocker']

bicho *m.* pud, penis ['bug']

bollo *m.* pussy, vagina ['bread roll, bun']

bufa *f.* fart

bufo *m.* fag, homosexual

buscona *f.* streetwalker, prostitute ['one who searches']

cabrón *m.* 1. cuckold 2. bastard, shitass *cf.* κερατάς
¡Cabrón! You bastard! *as an insult or humorously* βρε κερατά!
El muy cabrón le robó el caballo. That bastard stole his horse.

caca *f., child language* 1. shit 2. dirt
¡Caca! Don't touch! It's dirty!

cacada *f., var. of* cagada

cachar to ball, have sex with

cagada *f.* 1. shit 2. (act of) shitting 3. fuck-up, blunder
Eso es como cagadas de hormiga. This has no importance at all. ['this is like ant shit']
¡Él es la cagada! He's a real shit!
Su última película es una cagada. His last film is a real piece of shit.

cagadero *m.* outhouse, latrine

—13—

cagado 1. *m.* coward 2. *adj.* cowardly cf. χέστης
¡Francisco es un cagado! Francisco is a goddamned coward!

cagajón *m.* horse *or* mule shit

cagalera *f.* 1. the runs, diarrhea 2. fear
Él tiene cagalera. He's scared shitless.
¡Brava cagalera! What a hell of a mess!

cagaleta *f., var. of* cagalera

cagar 1. to shit 2. to dirty, soil 3. to fuck up, bungle
Tengo que cagar. I've got to take a shit.

cagarruta *f.* 1. sheep *or* cow shit 2. twerp, unimportant person

cagarse 1. to take a shit 2. to shit on oneself
¡Me cago en Diós! Hell! Goddammit! ['I shit on God']
¡Me cago en la puta Virgen! Goddammit! ['I shit on the whore Virgin Mary']
¡Me cago en la mar! Damn it! ['I shit in the sea']
¡Me cago en la leche de tu puta madre! You goddamned motherfucker! ['I shit in the milk of your whore mother']
¡Me cago en la leche de que mamaste! You cocksucking bastard! ['I shit in the milk you sucked']
¡Me cago en la hostia! Shit! Goddammit! ['I shit on the communion wafer']
Se cagó de miedo. He shit his pants from fear. χέστηκε απ' το φόβο

cagatintas *m.* office worker ['one who shits ink']

cagatorio *m., var. of* cagadero

cagón 1. *adj.* who shits profusely 2. *adj.* cowardly χέστης
3. *m.* child with diarrhea
¡Cagón de mierdas! You little shit! *said of a child*

cáguense *m.* last straw, limit
Esto es el cáguense. That's the last straw.

cagueta *f.* runny shit, diarrhea

caguetas *m.* 1. little child 2. coward χέστης
   ¡Eres un caguetas! You little turd! *said of a child*
capar to castrate
   Lo mandó a capar ratones. He told him to get the hell
   out. ['he sent him to castrate rats']
capullo 1. *m.* foreskin 2. *adj.* stupid ['cocoon; bud']
   ¡No seas capullo! Don't be stupid!
carajo *m.* 1. prick 2. motherfucker, bastard
   ¡Carajo! Fuck! Damn it! *expresses anger, annoyance*
   ¡Vete al carajo! Get fucked! Go to hell! ['go to the
   prick']
   ¡Adelante, carajos, echen bala! Come on, you moth-
   erfuckers, start shooting!
   ¡No me importa un carajo! I don't give a shit! ['I
   don't care a prick about it']
coger to fuck
cogienda *f.* (act of) fucking
cojones *m. pl.* balls, testicles
   No me importa dos cojones. I don't give a shit. ['I
   don't care two balls about it']
   ¡Cojones! Oh, bullshit! *expresses incredulity* cf. ἀρχίδια
   ¡Y un cojón! Like fuck it is! *expresses doubt about
   something said*
   ¡Me cago en los veinticuatro cojones de los apóstoles
   de Jesús! Goddamn it all to hell! ['I take a shit on
   the twenty-four testicles of the apostles of Jesus']
   Hace falta tener cojones. You've got to have balls
   (i.e., be brave).
   Es un tipo sin cojones. That guy's a fucking coward.
   ['he's a guy without balls']
cojonudo great, very good
   ¡Es un libro cojonudo! It's a damn good book!
cojudo gullible, stupid

colgantes *m. pl.* balls, testicles ['dangling things']

comer to eat (out), perform cunnilingus
Se la comió. He ate her out.

concha *f.* pussy, vagina ['(sea-)shell']

concho *m., var. of* concha

conejo *m.* pussy, vagina ['rabbit']

coña *f.* 1. cunt 2. joking (around), jesting
¡No me des la coña! Fuck off! ['don't give me the cunt']

coñazo *m.* boredom
¡Vaya coñazo! What a fucking bore!

coñearse to joke around

coño *m.* 1. cunt 2. stupid person
¡Coño! Shit! *expresses anger or surprise*
¡Coño! You fucking idiot!
¡Qué coño! Fuck! Damn it!
¡Vete al coño de tu madre! Fuck you! ['go to your mother's cunt']

correrse to come, have orgasm
Se hizo una paja hasta correrse. He jacked off until he came.
¡Me corrí de puro gusto! I was feeling damned good! ['I came from pure pleasure']

cuesco *m.* fart ['stone; punch']

culicagado *m.* little kid ['shit-covered ass']

culito *m.* (little) ass, small buttocks

Sana, sana,	Heal up, heal,
culito de rana,	frog's little ass,
si no sanas hoy,	if you don't heal today
sanarás mañana.	you'll be well tomorrow.

said to a child who has bumped himself

culo *m.* 1. ass, buttocks 2. ass-hole, anus 3. cunt *rare*
Le dio un puntapié en el culo. He kicked him in the ass.

Es un culo de mal asiento. He's fidgety. ['he has an
ass that won't sit right']
ir con el culo a rastras 1. to be in a jam 2. to be broke,
out of money ['to go with the ass dragging']
La ciudad va de culo. The city's going downhill. ['the
city is going on its ass']
lamer el culo *a alguien* to kiss *somebody's* ass, brown-
nose ['to lick the ass']
culón *adj.* having a big ass cf. κωλαράς
chingar 1. to fuck 2. to wear out, tire 3. to cheat,
swindle 4. to annoy, molest —cf. μᾶς γάμbες πιά!
¡Chinga tu madre! Fuck your mother!
¡A la chingada! Fuck it! Damn it!
chocho *m.* pussy, vagina ['floppy']
chorizo *m.* 1. prick 2. shit ['pork sausage']
chucha *f.* 1. cunt 2. armpit sweat
chumino *m.* pussy, vagina
chupar to blow, fellate
Me la chupó. She sucked me off.
churro *m.* 1. turd 2. prick ['fritter']
mojar el churro to ball, copulate with ['to wet the
fritter']
desbeber to piss ['to un-drink']
desocupar to shit ['to empty']
diligencia: hacer una diligencia *euph.* to answer the call
of nature, go to the bathroom ['to do an errand']
empalmarse to get a hard on/erection
Se me empalmó. I got a hard on.
favor: Nadie le ha hecho el favor. No one has made it
(i.e., had sex) with her. ['no one has done her the favor']
follar 1. to ball, have sex with 2. to fart silently ['to
blow with bellows']
Se la folló. He balled her.

follarse to fart silently

follón *m.* 1. silent fart 2. jam, mess ['noiseless rocket']
  ¡Vaya follón! What a fucked-up mess!
  Se metió en un follón. He got into a mess.

follonarse to fart silently

follonero *m.* treacherous, ungrateful person

goma *f.* rubber, condom

hideputa *m.* son of a bitch ['son of a whore']

hijoputa *m., var. of* hideputa
  ¡Ése es un hijoputa! That guy's a real son of a bitch!

hostia: ¡Me cago en la purimísima hostia! Fuck it all to
  hell! *expresses anger* ['I take a shit on the most holy
  communion wafer']

huevada *f.* stupid act, foolishness [*from* huevos 'balls']

huevón *adj.* 1. lazy 2. stupid ['having large balls']

huevos *m. pl.* balls, testicles ['eggs']
  ¡Me costó un huevo! That was a ball-buster! (i.e.,
    that was difficult). ['it cost me a ball']
  Él tiene huevos. He's got guts (he's brave). ['he has
    balls']
  Tengo más huevos que tú. I'm braver than you. ['I
    have more balls than you']

jiñar 1. to shit 2. to piss

joda *f.* 1. annoyance, bother 2. joke [*from* joder 'to
  fuck']
  Lo dijo en joda. He said it as a joke.

joder 1. to fuck 2. to annoy 3. to steal 4. to fuck up,
  fail
  ¡Joder! Fuck! *expresses annoyance, surprise*
  Esto me jode. I'm sick and tired of this fucking shit.
    ['this fucks me']
  Son ganas de joder. They're just trying to be a pain in
    the ass (i.e., to irritate).

¡No me jodas! Don't fuck around with me! ['don't fuck me']

Alguien les jodió el libro. Someone swiped their fucking book. ['someone fucked their book']

Se jodió todo. Everything got fucked up.

Se ha jodido la función. The show was a real fucking flop. ['the show got fucked']

¡Que te jodas! Fuck off! Get out of here! ['may you fuck yourself'] cf. ἄει γαμήσου!

¡Hay que joderse! This is the fucking end! To hell with it all! ['one should fuck oneself']

jodido *adj.* 1. exhausted 2. difficult 3. fucking, damned 4. ruined ['fucked']

Es un libro jodido. This book is goddamned hard to read.

Estoy jodido. I'm fucking tired.

No tengo ni una jodida peseta. I don't have a fucking cent.

Todo está jodido. Everything's fucked up.

jodienda *f.* pain in the ass, annoyance ['act of fucking']

jodón *adj.* 1. annoying 2. untrustworthy

jodontón *adj.* horny, desirous of sex

lagarta *f.* 1. whore 2. bitch, woman *abusive* ['lizard']

lambeculo *m. & f.* ass-kisser, sycophant ['one who licks ass'] cf. κωλογλύφτης

lameculos *m. & f.* ass-kisser, sycophant ['one who licks asses'] cf. κωλογλύφτης

leche *f.* come, semen ['milk']

¡Leche! 1. Fuck off! 2. Hell! *expresses anger*

Es un tío de mala leche. He's a mean motherfucker. ['he is a guy with spoiled come']

Hoy tiene mala leche. He's in a shitty mood today. ['he has spoiled come today']

Hay mucha mala leche entre ellos. There's a lot of bad feeling between them. ['there's a lot of bad come between them']

Aquí hay mucha mala leche. There's a lot of ill feeling around here. ['there's a lot of spoiled come here']

leñe *m., euph. for* leche

madre: ¡Tu madre! (Fuck) your mother! (*see* chingar); mentar la madre *a uno* to insult *someone* violently ['to mention *someone's* mother']

¡Eres un madre! You're a fucking coward! ['you're a mother']

mamada *f.* blow-job, fellatio

Me dio una mamada. She gave me a blow job.

mamar to suck, fellate

¡Que te la mame tu madre! You goddamned motherfucker! ['may your mother suck it for you']

Se la mamó. She blew him.

Me mamó la pinga. She sucked my cock.

mar *f., euph. for* madre *in obscene expressions*

margaritas *f. pl.* boobs, breasts ['pearls']

marica *m.* fag, homosexual

maricón *m.* fag, homosexual

Aquí hay mucho maricón. There are lots of fags here.

mariposa *m.* fag, homosexual ['butterfly']

meada *f.* 1. piss 2. piss stain 3. volume of urine excreted on one occasion [*from* mear 'to piss']

echar una meada to take a piss

meadero *m.* urinal

meado *m.* coward ['piss']

Es un meado. He's a yellow-bellied coward.

meado de la araña infected with V.D. ['spider's piss']

meados *m. pl.* piss

mear 1. to piss 2. to piss on

¡Si no te calles, te meo!   If you don't shut up, I'll piss on you!

mearse 1. to piss on oneself 2. to get away with, fool

Se meó de risa.   He laughed so hard he pissed his pants. *katουρήθηκε από τα γέλια.*

Se lo meó.   He pulled a fast one. He got away with it.

mecachis *euph. for* me cago (*see* cagarse)

¡Mecachis en la mar!   Darn it!

melocotones *m. pl.* boobs, breasts ['peaches']

meneársela to beat off, masturbate ['to shake it for oneself']

Se la menea todas las noches.   He whips it off every night.

meón *m. & f.* 1. bedwetter, pantswetter 2. newborn child [*from* mear 'to piss'] *cf. κατρουλά-ης, -ού*

mierda *f.* 1. shit 2. dirt, filth

¡Mierda!   Shit! *expresses annoyance, anger*

¡Es un(a) mierda!   He's a real shit!

Es un don Mierda.   He's a real nobody. ['he's a Mr. Shit']

¡Vete a la (mismísima) mierda!   Go fuck yourself! ['go right to the shit']

Todo estaba lleno de mierda.   There was crap everywhere (i.e., it was dirty). ['everything was full of shit']

Cogió una mierda.   He got shit-faced (i.e. drunk).

minga *f.* prick, penis

minina *f., child language* peter, penis ['kitty cat']

minino *m., child language* pussy, vagina ['kitty cat']

nabo *m.* dick, penis ['turnip']

ojete *m.* ass-hole, anus

ojo del culo *m.* ass-hole, anus ['eye of the ass']

paja: hacerse una/la paja to beat off, masturbate ['to do one's straw']

Se hizo una paja hasta correrse.   He beat off till he came.

palo *m.* rod, penis ['pole; stick']
echar un palo to screw, copulate with
Le echó un palo. He stuck it to her. ['he threw her a stick']
papaya *f.* pussy, vagina
pararse to have a hard on, have an erection
Se me paró. I got a hard on.
partes *f. pl.* privates (*euph. for* genitals)
pederse *var. of* peerse
pedo 1. *m.* fart 2. *m.* drunkenness 3. *adj.* ugly
Se tiró un pedo. He let a fart.
¡Vaya pedo! How ugly!
Es más fea que un pedo. She is damned ugly. ['she is uglier than a fart']
pedorrera *f.* (series of) farts
pedorrero 1. *adj.* farting frequently 2. *m.* one who farts κλανιάρ
peerse to fart
pelotas *f. pl.* balls, testicles ['balls']
tener pelotas to have guts, be brave ['to have balls']
pendeja *f.* whore
pendejada *f.* foolishness, stupidity
pendejarse to act like a fool
pendejo *m.* 1. pubic hair 2. stupid person
pendejear to act like a fool
pendona *f.* whore
pera: hacerse una/la pera to jack off, masturbate ['to make oneself a pear']
Se hizo una pera. He beat his meat.
pico *m.* prick, penis ['beak']
picha *f.* cock, penis
pichada *f.* (act of) screwing, copulation
Hace mucho tiempo que no tengo una pichada. It's been a long time since I've been laid.

pichar to screw, copulate
Vamos a pichar. Let's have a screw.
pija *f.* 1. prick, penis 2. stupid person
Es un(a) pija. He's a fucking idiot. ['he is a prick']
pinga *f.* cock, penis
pingo *m.* slut, whore
pingona *f.* whore
pipí *m., child language* pee, urine
hacer pipí to go wee-wee, urinate
pito *m.* prick ['horn, whistle']
polvete *m., var. of* polvo
polvo *m.* (act of) screwing ['powder']
echar un polvo to ball, fuck ['to throw a powder']
Le echó un polvo. He balled/humped her.
polla *f.* prick, penis ['young chicken'] cf. Rum. pulă
ponerse dura to get a hard on, have an erection
Se me puso dura. I got a hard on.
porra *f.* prick, penis ['club, bludgeon']
puñeta *f.* (act of) beating off, masturbation
hacer puñetas to beat off
Lo mandó a hacer puñetas. He told him to fuck off.
  ['he sent him to jack off']
¡Puñeta! *or* ¡Qué puñetas! Oh, fuck!
¡Vaya puñeta! What a fucked-up mess! ['what jack-
  ing-off']
¡Vete a hacer puñetas! Fuck off! ['go beat off']
purgación *f.* 1. period, menstruation 2. clap, gonorrhea ['purging']
tener purgaciones to have the clap
puta *f.* whore
puta callejera streetwalker
casa de putas whorehouse
ir de putas to go whoring

—23—

hijo de puta   son of a bitch

¡Me cago en la leche de tu puta madre!   You goddamned motherfucker!   ['I shit in the milk of your
whore mother']

putada *f.* annoyance

¡Me hizo una putada!   He bugged the shit out of me!

puto *m.* son of a bitch

raja *f.* pussy, vagina   ['slit, crack']

seta *f.* box, vagina   ['mushroom']

tetas *f. pl.* tits

tetona *f.* woman with big tits

tirarse to screw, have sex with

Se la tiró.   He put it to her.

tortilla *f.* lesbian sex

tortillera *f.* lesbian   ['tortilla vendor']

tragar 1. to ball, have sex with 2. to sleep around, be
promiscuous

Tragaban toda la noche.   They were balling all night.

traque *m.* loud fart   ['crack, bang']

tumbar to lay, have sex with   ['to knock down']

vaina *f.* 1. pussy, vagina 2. (act of) screwing   ['sheath,
scabbard']

verga *f.* 1. cock, penis 2. stupid person

Es una verga.   He's a stupid prick.

zulla *f.* crap, feces

zullarse 1. to dirty oneself 2. to fart

zullón *m.* fart

zurullo *m.* turd   ['hard lump']

zurullón *m.* turd   ['hard lump']

ITALIAN

bocchino *m.* blow job, fellatio ['mouthpiece, ciga-
ette holder']
  Lei gli ha fatto un bocchino. She gave him a blow job.
cacadubbi *m. & f.* wishy-washy, indecisive person ['one
who shits doubts']
cacare to shit
cacarella *f.* 1. the runs, diarrhea 2. fright
cacarsi to shit on oneself
  cacarsi sotto 1. to shit one's pants 2. to be a coward
  ['to shit on oneself underneath']
  Mi sono cacato sotto. 1. I shit my pants. 2. I was
  scared shitless. *cf.* Τὰ 'κατα (ἐ)πάνω μου.
cacasangue *m.* dysentery ['shitting blood']
  used mainly in the curse: Ti venga il cacasangue! May
  you get dysentery! (i.e., may misfortune befall you)
cacasenno *m.* smart aleck ['one who shits wisdom']
cacasodo *m. & f.* conceited person ['one who shits
hard']
cacasotto *m.* 1. coward 2. clumsy person ['one who χέστης
shits underneath']
cacastecchi *m.* miser ['one who shits twigs']
cacata *f.* (act of) shitting
  fare una cacata 1. to take a shit 2. to fuck up, bungle
  Ho fatto una cacata. 1. I took a shit. 2. I fucked up.
cacatoio *m.* latrine

cacatura 1. shit 2. *var. of* cacata

cacca *f.* 1. shit 2. dirt (in general) 3. arrogance, pride
  aver la cacca al culo to be scared shitless, be terrified
  ['to have shit on the ass']
  Cacca! Oh, shit! *expresses anger, annoyance*

cacchiata *f.* 1. fuck-up, mistake 2. *euph. for* cazzata

cacchio *m., euph. for* cazzo
  Cacchio! Shit! Damn it! *expresses anger, annoyance*

caccola *f.* 1. "sleep", mucus in eyes 2. snot, nasal
  mucus

cacone *m.* 1. person who shits frequently 2. coward

cagare *var. of* cacare
  Non mi caga neanche. She doesn't give a shit about
  me. ['she doesn't even shit (on) me']

cavolo *m., euph. for* cazzo ['cabbage']
  Non capisco un cavolo! I don't understand a frigging
  thing!

cazzata *f.* 1. stupidity, foolishness 2. chewing-out,
  scolding 3. dirty trick [*from* cazzo]
  M'ha fatto una cazzata. 1. He really chewed my ass
  out. 2. He played a dirty fucking trick on me.

cazzo *m.* 1. prick 2. affair, matter
  Fatti i cazzi tuoi! Mind your own fucking business!
  ['make your own pricks']
  Non rompermi il cazzo! Don't fuck around with me!
  Don't bother me! ['don't break my prick']
  Chi cazzo se ne frega? Who the fuck gives a shit?
  Non capisco un cazzo! I don't understand a fucking
  thing! ['I don't understand a prick']
  Non ha detto un cazzo! He didn't say a fucking thing!
  testa di cazzo ass-hole, bastard ['prick head']
  del cazzo worthless, no-good ['of the prick']
  È un film del cazzo! That film is a piece of shit!

col cazzo! *or* un cazzo! Fuck no! *expresses surprise,
anger, emphatic rejection* ['with the prick' *or* 'a prick']
Cazzo! Shit! *expresses anger, annoyance*
cazzo duro   hard on, erection   ['hard prick']
avere il cazzo duro   to have a hard on

> Acqua fresca, vino puro   Fresh water, pure wine
> fica stretta, cazzo duro   tight cunt, hard cock
> *(popular answer to the question: "what are the
> most necessary things in life?")*

cazzomatto *m.* stupid person ['prick-crazy']

cazzottare to beat up [*from* cazzo]

cazzottarsi to (get into a) fight

Si sono cazzottati per le vie. They were beating the
shit out of each other on the street.

cazzottata *f., var. of* cazzottatura

cazzottatura *f.* (act of) beating

Ha ricevuto una solenne cazzottatura. He got the holy
fucking shit beat out of him.

cazzotto *m.* a hard punch/blow

L'ho preso a cazzotti. I knocked the shit out of him.

chiappa *f.* cheek, buttock [*from* chiappare 'to grab,
sieze']

Lei ha delle belle chiappe! She's got a nice ass!

chiavare to screw, copulate with ['to nail, pierce']

coglia *f.* 1. scrotum, balls 2. fop, fancy dresser

cogliata *f.* boastful remark

cogliona *f.* stupid woman [*from* coglione]

coglionaggine *f.* stupidity, foolishness

coglionare to ridicule, mock

coglionata *f., var. of* coglioneria

coglionatore *m.* person who ridicules

coglionatura *f.* mockery, ridicule

coglione *m.* 1. ball, testicle 2. stupid person

Non rompermi i coglioni! Don't fuck around with me! Don't bother me! ['don't break my balls']

Questo tizio ha i coglioni duri (*or* quadrati). That guy is a tough motherfucker. ['that guy has hard (*or* square) balls']

levarsi *qc.* dai coglioni to get rid of *smb.* ['to lift *smb.* off one's balls']

Mi sono levato Giovanni dai coglioni! I got rid of that fucking Giovanni! ['I lifted Giovanni off my balls']

Levati dai coglioni! Get the fuck out of here! ['lift yourself off my balls']

Quel coglione di tuo padre! Your father's a fucking idiot! *general insult*

Mi sta sui coglioni. He's a real pain in the ass. ['he's standing on my balls']

Non me ne sbatto i coglioni! I don't give a flying fuck about it! ['I don't beat my balls over it']

coglioneria *f.* 1. foolish act 2. stupidity 3. trifle

culo *m.* 1. ass, buttocks 2. ass-hole, anus 3. good luck

Vai a fare in culo! (*often pronounced* va fa 'n culo) Go get fucked! ['go get yourself fucked in the ass']

Vai a fartelo mettere in culo! Go get fucked! ['go get it put to you in the ass']

Che culo! What luck!

fare il culo rosso (*or* nero) a *qc.* to beat the shit out of *smb.* ['to make *someone's* ass red (*or* black)']

prendere *qc.* per il culo 1. to make a fool of *smb.* 2. to cheat *smb.* ['to take *smb.* by the ass(-hole)']

L'ho preso per il culo. I fooled the hell out of him.

In culo alla ballena! Good luck! ['up the whale's ass'] *used among students to wish success on exams; the popular reply is* che non scorregi! 'I hope it doesn't fart!'

ditalino *m.* (female) masturbation ['little thimble']
  farsi un ditalino to masturbate ['to do a little thimble on oneself']

fica *f.* 1. cunt 2. woman *derogatory*
  Che fica! What a piece of ass!
  fare le fiche to flip *smb.* off, give *smb.* the finger (*see also* figa)

ficona *f.* 1. whore 2. sexy woman ['big cunt']

figa *f., var. of* fica

finocchio *m.* fag, homosexual ['fennel']

fottere 1. to fuck 2. to fuck (over), cheat, swindle
  Vai a farti fottere! Go get fucked! Go to hell!

fottersi not to care
  fottersi di *qc./q.c.* not to care about *smb./smth.*
  Me ne fotto di lui! I don't give a fuck about him!
  Me ne fotto di soldi. I don't give a fuck about money.

fottìo *m.* large amount, large number [*from* fottere]
  C'era un fottìo di gente. There was a hell of a fucking lot of people there.
  Ha un fottìo di soldi. He's got a shitload of money.

fottuto 1. fucked (*past participle of* fottere) 2. goddamned, fucking, no-good 3. ruined, lost
  Sono fottuto! I'm done for, ruined! ['I'm fucked']

fregare 1. to hump, copulate with 2. to screw (over), cheat 3. to swipe, steal ['to rub']

fregarsi not to care
  fregarsi di *qc./q.c.* not to care about *smb./smth.*
  Che te ne frega!? What the fuck do you care!?
  Me ne frego dei suoi ordini! I don't give a shit about your orders!
  Chi se ne frega? Who gives a shit?
  Non me ne frega niente! I don't give a flying fuck!

fregata *f.* 1. (act of) screwing, copulating 2. swindle,

cheat   [*from* fregare]
Ti hanno dato una fregata. You've been screwed (i.e. cheated).

fregatura *f.* 1. swindle, cheat   2. wash-out, failure 3. nuisance [*from* fregar]
È una bella fregatura! This is a fine fucking mess!
Questa pioggia è una grossa fregatura! This rain is a royal fucking pain in the ass!

fregna *f.* 1. cunt 2. gossip, lies 3. trouble, nuisance
Non raccontar fregne! Don't give me that bullshit! ['don't tell cunts']
aver le fregne to be worried, depressed ['to have the cunts']
La fregna di tua sorella! 1. *insulting remark* 2. Goddammit! *expresses anger* ['your sister's cunt']

fregniacciaro *m.* bullshitter, liar [*from* fregna]

frigna *f., var. of* fregna

froscio *m.* fag, homosexual

grilletto *m.* clit, clitoris ['trigger']

guanto *m.* rubber, condom ['glove']

incazzarsi to get pissed off, become angry [*from* cazzo]

incazzato *adj.* pissed off, angry

leccaculi *m. & f., var. of* leccaculo

leccaculo *m. & f.* ass-kisser, sycophant ['one who licks ass']

leccata *f.* cunnilingus ['licking']
Le ha fatto una leccata. He ate her out.
Al direttore ha fatto una leccata di culo. He brownnosed the director. ['he gave the director a licking on the ass']

loffa *f.* (noiseless) fart

merda *f.* 1. shit 2. dirt (in general) 3. shitass, bastard
Lui è una merda! He's a real shit(ass)!

Merda! Shit! *expresses annoyance, anger, refusal*

merdaio *m.* 1. pile of shit 2. filthy place

merdata *f.* 1. stupidity 2. fuck-up, failure, mess

merdone *m.* 1. sloppy person 2. person who shits frequently 3. coward

merdoso *adj.* 1. covered with shit 2. filthy 3. damned, no-good

mignotta *f.* whore
figlio d'una mignotta son of a bitch

minchia *f.* 1. cock, penis 2. fool 3. cunt

minchionaggine *f.* stupidity, foolishness

minchionare to trick, fool

minchione 1. *m.* ball, testicle 2. *m.* fool 3. *adj.* foolish, stupid
Minchione! Damn it!
rompere i minchioni to bug, be a pest ['to break the balls']

minchioneria *f.* stupidity

mona *f.* pussy, vagina
Vai in mona! Fuck off! Get out of here! ['go to (a) cunt']
Vai in mona di tua sorella! Get the fuck out of here! ['go to your sister's cunt']

palla *f.* ball, testicle ['ball']
Non rompermi le palle! Stop fucking around with me! ['don't break my balls']
L'esame m'ha rotto le palle. I really fucked up on the exam. ['the exam broke my balls']
Palle! Shit! Balls! *expresses anger, surprise* ['balls']

patacca *f.* pussy, vagina ['a coin of little value']

peto *m.* fart

pipì *f., child language* 1. pee, urine 2. peter, penis
fare pipì to wee-wee, urinate

Il piccolo deve fare pipì.   The child has to pee.

Mi scappa la pipì.   I'm dying to pee.

pipa *f.*   1. masturbation   2. blow job, fellatio   ['pipe']

farsi una pipa   to beat off, masturbate   ['to do a pipe on oneself']

Ieri si è fatto una pipa tre volte.   He jacked off three times yesterday.

Lei gli ha fatto una bella pipa.   She gave him a terrific blow job.

Vatti a fare una pipa!   Fuck off!   Get out of here! ['go jack off']

piscia *f.*   piss, urine

pisciadura *f., var. of* pisciatura

pisciagione *m.*   piss, urine

pisciaia *f.*   insignificant affair

È una pisciaia.   It doesn't amount to (a crock of) shit.

piscialetto *m. & f.*   little kid, child   ['one who pisses in the bed']

pisciare   1. to piss   2. to leak   3. to spout, spurt   4. to waste, spend

un recipiente che piscia acqua da ogni parte   a container that leaks everywhere

pisciare denari   to waste money   ['to piss money']

Questo tizio li ha pisciati via.   That guy blew all his money.   ['that guy pissed it all away']

Mi scappa di pisciare.   I can't wait to take a piss.

pisciare sangue   1. to piss blood   2. to sweat blood, work hard

Tu parla quando pisciano le galline!   Keep your damn mouth shut!   ['talk when the chickens piss']

pisciarci sopra   to despise, scorn   ['to piss on']

A Giovanni non importano buoni voti. Ci piscia sopra. Giovanni doesn't care about good grades. He doesn't give a shit about them.   ['he pisses on them']

pisciarsi   to piss on oneself

pisciarsi addosso   to piss one's pants   ['to piss on one-self']

pisciarsi sotto   to piss one's pants (from fear)   ['to piss on oneself underneath']

pisciasotto   *m.*   1. one who pisses his pants 2. coward ['one who pisses under himself']

pisciatoio   *m.*   1. public urinal 2. smelly place

pisciata   *f.*   1. (act of) pissing 2. volume of urine excreted on one occasion 3. long, drawn-out speech

fare una pisciata   to take a piss

pisciatura   *f.*   (act of) pissing

piscio   *m., var. of* piscia

piscione   *m.*   1. one who pisses his pants 2. baby, child

piscioso   *adj.*   covered with piss

pisciutella   *f.*   pussy, vagina   [*from* pisciare 'to piss']

pomiciare   to pet, feel up

pompiciare   *var. of* pomiciare

pompino   *m.*   blow job, fellatio   [*from* pompare 'to pump']

Lei gli ha fatto un pompino.   She gave him a blow job.

puttana   *f.*   whore

Madonna puttana!   *expresses anger, surprise*   ['that whore Virgin Mary']

quaglia   *f.*   box, pussy, vagina   ['quail']

recchione   *m.*   fag, homosexual   ['big ears']

rincoglionirsi   1. to become senile 2. to become stupid [*from* coglione 'testicle']

Quel rincoglionito di tuo nonno!   *insulting remark* ['what an old fool your grandfather is']

rizzarsi   to have a hard on, have an erection

Mi si è rizzato.   I have a hard on.   ['mine is standing

erect']

rompicoglioni *m., var. of* rompipalle ['ball-breaker']

rompipalle *m.* 1. ball-buster, cruel person 2. pain in the ass, bothersome person ['ball-breaker']

sbattere to screw, copulate with ['to knock, bang']

sbattersi not to care

Me lo sbatto. I don't give a shit. ['I screw it']

sburro *m.* come, semen [*from* sburrare 'to skim milk']

scopare to ball, copulate with ['to sweep']

Chi scopa bene, She who knows how to ball (sweep),
Trova buon marito. finds a good husband.

scopata *f.* (act of) balling, sexual intercourse

fare una scopata to (get a) fuck

Ho fatto una scopata. I got laid.

scopona *f.* 1. cheap whore 2. easy lay, promiscuous woman [*from* scopare]

scoreggia *f.* (noisy) fart

fare una scoreggia to let a fart

scoreggiare to fart (noisily)

sega *f.* jacking off, masturbation ['saw']

farsi una sega *or* fare la sega to beat off ['to do a saw on oneself']

Si è fatto una sega. He beat his meat.

Non ne sa una sega. He doesn't know a fucking thing.

segaiuolo *m.* jerk-off, person who masturbates to excess

segata *f.* fuck-up, mistake, mess

Ha fatto una segata. He really fucked up.

stronzetto *m., dim. of* stronzo

stronzino *m., dim. of* stronzo

stronzo *m.* 1. turd, piece of shit 2. stupid, inept person

Non voglio più sentir parlare di quello stronzo! I don't want to hear any more talk about that stupid ass-hole!

stronzolo *m.* turd, piece of shit

succhiotto *m.* blow job, fellatio ['pacifier']

sveltino *m.* quick masturbation session [*from* svelto 'quick']

Si è fatto uno sveltino. He did a "quickie" on himself.

tette *f. pl.* tits

uccellino *m., var. of* uccello

uccello *m.* dick, penis ['bird']

venire *said of men and women* to come, have orgasm

Sono venuto tre volte. I came three times.

FRENCH

anglais *m. pl.* (menstrual) period ['English']
Elle a ses anglais. She's on the rag. ['she's having her English']

avoir to lay, have, copulate with ['to have']
Il l'a eue. He made it with her. He had her.

baisage *m.* (act of) fucking

baiser 1. to fuck 2. to catch (an illness) 3. to fool, deceive 4. to arrest 5. to steal [*the original meaning of* baiser, *'to kiss', is usually expressed now by* embrasser]
Elle baise bien. She's a good fuck.

baiseur *m.* man who fucks

baiseuse *f.* woman who fucks
Elle est une sacrée baiseuse. She's a hell of a good fuck.

baisodrome *m., hum.* 1. whorehouse 2. bedroom ["fuckodrome"]

balle: trou de balle *m.* 1. ass-hole, anus 2. stupid person ['bullet hole']

bandant *adj.* sexually exciting [*from* bander]
C'est bandant. That's a real turn-on.

bander 1. to have a hard on/erection 2. to be horny, be sexually excited

bandeur *m.* man obsessed with sex

bandeuse *f.* prick tease(r), woman who teases sexually

bite *f.* prick, penis ['vertical post']

biter to screw, copulate with [*from* bite]

bitte *f., var. of* bite

branlage *f.* (act of) masturbation [*from* branler]

branler: se branler to beat off, masturbate ['to shake oneself']

    s'en branler not to care about

    Je m'en branle. I don't give a shit about it. ['I beat off over it']

    se les branler to fuck around, loaf

branleur *m.* 1. masturbator 2. fuck-off, lazy person

caca *m., child language* 1. doo-doo, excrement 2. dirt (in general)

    faire caca to crap, defecate

capote anglaise *f.* rubber, condom ['English bonnet']

carte *f.* wet dream, nocturnal emission ['map']

    faire une carte to have a wet dream ['to paint a map']

casse-cul *m.* boring person ['ass-breaker']

casse-couilles *m.* boring person ['ball-breaker']

chat *m.* pussy, vagina ['cat']

chatte *f., var. of* chat ['(female) cat']

chaude-pisse *f.* clap, gonorrhea ['hot piss']

chiasse *f.* 1. the runs, diarrhea 2. insect shit

    avoir la chiasse 1. to have the runny shits 2. to be scared

    Ça me donne la chiasse. That scares the shit out of me. ['that gives me the runny shits']

chiée *f.* large amount [*from* chier]

    Il a une chiée d'argent. He's got a shitload of money.

chier to shit

    Ça va chier dur! The shit's going to hit the fan! ['it's going to shit hard']

    Va te faire chier! Fuck off! Get out! ['go take a shit']

    Tu me fais chier! You bore my ass off! ['you make me shit']

Ça ne chie pas!   That doesn't make any fucking difference   ['that doesn't shit']

On se fait chier ici.   This place is goddamned boring!

Je l'ai envoyé chier.   I told him to fuck off.   ['I sent
him to take a shit']

chierie *f.* nuisance, bother
Quelle chierie!   What a pain in the ass!

chinois *m.* dong, penis   ['Chinese']

chtouille *f.* clap, gonorrhea

compisser to piss (on)

con 1. *m.* cunt 2. *m.* foolish person 3. *m.* bullshit, nonsense 4. *adj.* stupid, foolish
Espèce de con!   You fucking idiot!
à la con 1. badly made 2. silly, stupid
faire le con to act like a fool
Il est con comme la lune!   He's a real fucking moron!
le roi des cons an absolute idiot   ['the king of cunts']
C'est drôlement con!   That's just bullshit!

con(n)ard 1. *m.* stupid person 2. *adj.* stupid [*from* con
'cunt']
Elle est connarde.   She's damned stupid.

con(n)asse *f.* 1. bitch, woman *abusive* 2. whore 3. stupid person

conchier to shit (on)

conne 1. *f.* stupid woman 2. *adj., f.* stupid (*see* con 4)
une histoire conne a stupid story

conneau *m.* fool

connerie *f.* 1. bullshit, nonsense 2. fuck-up, stupid act
Ne dis pas des conneries!   Don't (talk) bullshit!
Tout ça c'est des conneries.   That's just a bunch of
bullshit.
faire des conneries to fuck up, blunder

coucher to have sex with   ['to go to bed']

coucherie *f.* sexual intercourse

couille *f.* ball, testicle

Il n'a pas de couilles. He has no balls/backbone (i.e., he's weak, soft, cowardly).

couille molle chicken, coward ['soft ball']

Il me casse les couilles. He bores my ass off. ['he breaks my balls']

en avoir plein les couilles to be tired of *smth.*

J'en ai plein les couilles de ces films! I'm fucking fed up with these movies! ['I have my balls full of these movies']

partir en couilles to go to pot, go downhill

couillon 1. *m.* ball, testicle 2. *m.* stupid person 3. *m., chiefly Southern France* buddy, friend 4. *adj.* stupid, foolish

faire le couillon to act like a fool

Il est un peu couillon. He's a bit dumb.

couillonnade *f.* 1. bullshit, nonsense 2. fuck-up, stupid act

couillonner 1. to make a fool of 2. to fuck around, fool around

cul *m.* 1. ass, buttocks 2. stupid person

trou du cul *m.* ass-hole, anus ['ass-hole']

lecher le cul *à qn.* to kiss *smb's* ass, flatter ['to lick *smb's* ass']

en avoir plein le cul to be tired of *smth.*

J'en ai plein le cul! I'm goddamned tired of this! ['I have my ass full of it']

péter plus haut que le cul to put on airs ['to fart higher than one's ass']

Quel cul! What a stupid ass!

cyclope *m.* dick, penis ['cyclops']

faire pleurer le cyclope to come, ejaculate ['to make

the cyclops cry']

décharger to come, ejaculate ['to discharge, unload']

déconnage *m.* bullshit, nonsense [*from* con 'cunt']

déconner to talk bullshit/nonsense [*from* con 'cunt']

démerder to help *smb.* out of a difficult situation ['to pull out of the shit']

    Démerde-toi! Get the fuck out of here!

emmerdant *adj.* 1. boring, tedious 2. annoying, troublesome ['shitting on']

    Tu es emmerdant! You're a pain in the ass!

emmerdement *m.* bore, annoyance, bother ['act of shitting on']

    Quel emmerdement! What a fucking pain in the ass!

emmerder 1. to shit on 2. to bore 3. to annoy, bother

    Je l'emmerde! Fuck him! ['I shit on him']

    Je t'emmerde, à pied, à cheval et en voiture! Go fuck yourself in the ass! ['I shit on you on foot, on horseback, and in the car']

    Tu m'emmerdes! You bore my ass off!

    s'emmerder to be bored

    Il s'emmerde ici. He's fucking bored here.

emmerdeur *m.* annoying/boring person

emmerdeuse *f.* annoying/boring woman

enculage *m.* (act of) fucking in the ass, buggery

    enculage de mouches hairsplitting, quibbling ['fucking flies in the ass']

enculé *m.* 1. passive homosexual 2. shitass, bastard ['fucked in the ass']

enculer to fuck (in the ass) [*from* cul]

    Va te faire enculer! Get the fuck out of here! ['go get fucked in the ass']

enculeur *m.* active homosexual [*from* enculer]

    enculeur de mouches quibbler, hairsplitter ['one who

fucks flies in the ass']

foutaise *f.* trifle, unimportant matter [*from* foutre]

foutoir *m.* 1. whorehouse 2. mess, disorder [*from* foutre]

foutre 1. to do 2. to hit 3. to give 4. to stick, thrust [*original meaning* 'to fuck']

Va te faire foutre! Get your butt out of here! ['go get fucked']

Qu'est-ce que vous foutez là? What the hell are you up to?

Qu'est-ce que ça fout? Who the hell cares?

Ça ne fout rien! It doesn't matter a goddamned bit!

foutre le camp to beat it, run off

foutre la paix *à qn.* to leave *smb.* alone, not disturb *smb.*

se foutre not to care

Je m'en fous! I don't give a goddamn!

Je m'en fous et m'en contrefous! I don't give a flying fuck!

foutre *m.* come, semen

Foutre! Fuck! Shit! Goddammit! *expresses surprise, admiration, anger*

Foutre non! Hell no!

foutrer to come, ejaculate

foutu *adj.* 1. rotten, awful 2. done for, finished

Elle est bien foutue. She's built like a brick shithouse (i.e., has a shapely figure).

gouine *f.* lesbian

jouir to come, have orgasm ['to enjoy']

joyeuses *f. pl.* balls, testicles ['the ones which bring joy']

jus *m.* come, semen ['juice, gravy']

juter to come, have orgasm ['to give juice']

lèche-cul *m.* ass-kisser, flatterer ['one who licks ass']

Marie-couche-toi-là *f.* an easy lay, promiscuous woman ['Marie-go-right-to-bed']

merde *f.* 1. shit 2. crap, worthless object 3. shitass, bastard

Nous sommes dans la merde. We're up shit creek (i.e. we're in trouble). ['we're in the shit']

Merde! Shit! *expresses anger, dislike*

Merde (alors)! Wow! *expresses surprise, admiration*

Il ne se prend pas pour une merde. He thinks his shit doesn't stink (i.e., he has a high opinion of himself). ['he doesn't take himself for a shit']

de merde worthless, no good

Bon Dieu de merde! What the fuck! *expresses anger, surprise* ['good God of shit']

merdeux 1. *adj.* shitty, filthy 2. *m.* turd, bastard 3. *m.* snot-nosed kid, brat

bâton merdeux shitass ['shit-covered stick']

merdier *m.* 1. pile of shit 2. fucked-up situation, confusion, disorder

merdoyer to be at a loss for words

nichon *m.* tit, breast

niquer to bang, copulate with

ordure *f.* shitass, bastard ['dung']

Fous-moi le camp, ordure! Get the fuck out of here, you shitass!

pédale *f.* pederast ['pedal']

peloter to feel up, pet, neck

pet *m.* fart

faire / lâcher un pet to let a fart

Ça ne vaut pas un pet de lapin. That isn't worth shit. ['that isn't worth a rabbit's fart']

pet de nonne *a kind of fritter* ['nun's fart']

pétarade *f.* 1. (series of) farts 2. (series of) explosions

péter 1. to fart 2. to bang, explode

Cette affaire va vous péter dans la main. That business of yours is going to get screwed up. ['your business is going to fart in your hand']

péter plus haut que le cul to be pretentious ['to fart higher than one's ass']

Ça va péter des flammes. All hell is going to break loose. ['that's going to fart flames']

Je l'ai envoyé péter. I sent him packing. ['I sent him to fart']

Il péte du feu *or* des flammes. He's a ball of fire, he's a real go-getter. ['he's farting fire *or* flames']

pète-sec *m.* grumpy, tyrannical person ['one who lets dry farts']

péteur *m.* 1. one who farts 2. coward ['farter']

péteuse *f.* 1. woman who farts 2. cowardly woman ['farter']

péteux *m., var. of* péteur

pied: prendre son pied to come, ejaculate

pine *f.* prick, penis

pipe: prendre la pipe to blow, perform fellatio ['to take the pipe']

prise de pipe blow-job, fellatio ['taking the pipe']

pipi *m., child language* pee, urine

faire pipi to wee-wee, urinate

pipi de chat rotgut, inferior wine ['cat pee']

pisse *f.* piss

pisse-froid *m.* cold fish, antisocial person ['one who has cold piss']

pissement *m.* (act of) pissing

pisser 1. to piss 2. to leak, spout

C'est comme si on pissait dans un violon. It was a waste of energy. ['it was as if one were pissing into a violin']

Je l'ai envoyé pisser. I told him to get the hell out. ['I sent him to take a piss']

faire pisser *qn.* to make *smb.* laugh hard ['to make *smb.* piss']

laisser pisser les mérinos to bide one's time ['to let the sheep piss']

Il pleut comme vache qui pisse. It's raining like a bastard (very hard). ['it's raining like a pissing cow']

Il y a de quoi pisser. That's pretty funny. ['there's something to piss about']

Sa bouche pisse le sang. The blood is flowing out of his mouth. ['his mouth is pissing blood']

se pisser to piss one's pants (*usually* from laughter)

pisseur *m.* one who pisses often

pisseur de copie hack (writer) ['one who pisses out pages']

pisseuse *f.* 1. woman who pisses often 2. little girl

pisseux *adj.* stained with *or* smelling of piss

pisse-vinaigre *m.* miser ['one who pisses vinegar']

pissoir *m.* urinal

pissotière *f.* (public) urinal

plume: tailler une plume to give a blow-job, perform fellatio ['to trim a feather']

polichinelle: avoir une polichinelle dans le tiroir to be knocked-up, be pregnant ['to have a puppet in the drawer']

pompier: faire un pompier to give a blow job, perform fellatio

putain *f.* 1. whore 2. promiscuous woman

Quel putain de temps! What shitty weather!

fils de putain son of a bitch

Putain! Shit! Wow! *expresses surprise*

putassier *adj.*   pertaining to a whore

pute *f., var. of* putain

queue *f.*   prick, penis ['tail']

quéquette *f.*   dick, penis ['little tail']

roulée: Elle est bien roulée! She's really stacked! (i.e., she has large breasts)

sucer   to blow, perform fellatio ['to suck']

tante *f.*   pederast ['aunt']

tapette *f.*   passive homosexual ['carpet beater']

voiles: marcher à voiles et à vapeur   to be AC/DC, be bisexual ['to navigate by sail and steam']

GERMAN

Unless otherwise noted, nouns are given in the nominative singular, followed by the genitive singular and nominative plural (if one exists). The principal parts of the unprefixed strong verbs are provided.

abspritzen to come, ejaculate ['to spray off']

Affenarsch, -es, ⁻e *m.* ass-hole, bastard ['ape-ass']
Sein Gesicht glänzt wie ein Affenarsch. His face is shining like an ape's ass. *said of a person who is drunk or who has oily skin*

Affenschwanz, -es, ⁻e *m.* 1. fop, dandy 2. fool ['ape-prick']

angestochen knocked-up, pregnant ['pricked, pierced']

anscheißen to chew out, reprimand severely ['to shit on']
Mein Boß hat mich angeschissen. My boss really chewed my ass out.

Anschiß, -es, -e *m.* cussing out, reprimand ['a shitting on']
Ich habe einen Anschiß von dem Bullen bekommen. That cop really raked me over the coals.

Arsch, -es, ⁻e *m.* 1. ass, buttocks 2. ass-hole, bastard
Leck mich am Arsch! Kiss my ass! Go to hell! ['lick me on the ass']
Du hast wohl 'n Arsch offen. You've got a screw loose. You're crazy. ['you have your ass open']
Du bist ein Arsch! You're an ass-hole!
Arsch mit Ohren ass, stupid person ['ass with ears']
den Arsch hängen lassen to be down in the mouth, be depressed ['to let one's ass hang']

am Arsch der Welt in the boondocks ['on the ass of the world']

jm. **in den Arsch kriechen** to brownnose, flatter ['to crawl into *someone's* ass']

Es ist im Arsch. It's gone to pot. ['it's in the ass']

Arschbacke, -, -en *f.* bun, buttock ['ass-cheek']

die Arschbacken zusammenklemmen to brace oneself ['to squeeze one's ass-cheeks together']

Arschficker, -s, - *m.* 1. fag, homosexual 2. ass-hole, fool ['ass-fucker']

Arschgeige, -, -n *f.* ass-hole, bastard ['ass-fiddle']

Arschgesicht, -s, -er *n.* stupid, ugly face ['ass-face']

Arschkipf, -es, -e *m.* ass-hole, bastard ['ass-croissant']

Arschkriecher, -s, - *m.* brownnose, flatterer ['ass-crawler']

Arschkriecherei, - *f.* brownnosing, sycophancy ['ass-crawling']

ärschlings assbackwards, clumsily

Arschwisch, -es, -e *m.* toilet paper ['ass-mop']

Arschloch, -es, ¨er *n.* 1. ass-hole, anus 2. ass-hole, bastard

Sein Arschloch ist zugeschnappt. He kicked the bucket (i.e., he died). ['his ass-hole has snapped shut']

aufreißen, riß auf, aufgerissen to make it with, have sex with ['to rip open']

Balkon: Sie hat einen grossen Balkon. She's well-stacked (has large breasts). ['she has a large balcony']

bepissen to piss (on)

bescheißen, bescheiß, beschissen 1. to shit on 2. to fuck over, cheat, swindle

Das Arschloch hat mich ganz schön beschissen! That ass-hole really fucked me over!

Beschiß, -es *m.* swindle, cheat ['a shitting on']

So ein Beschiß! What a lousy fucking trick!

beschissen 1. shit-covered 2. damned, lousy

Es geht ihm beschissen. He's having a lousy fucking time.

blasen, blies, geblasen to blow, fellate ['to blow']

Sie hat ihm einen geblasen. She gave him a blow job. ['she blew one for him']

bügeln to screw, have sex with ['to iron, press']

Er bügelt sie jede Nacht. He screws her every night.

bumsen to screw, have sex with ['to bang, bump']

Dreckscheiße, - *f.* shit, junk ['crap-shit']

Dünnpfiff, -es, -e *m.* the runs, diarrhea ['thin-whistle']

Dünnschiß, -es, -e *m.* runny shits, diarrhea ['thin-shit']

Heute habe ich Dünnschiß. I've got the runny shits today.

durchficken 1. to fuck (thoroughly) 2. to fuck (for a long time)

Sie muß mal richtig durchgefickt werden. What she needs is a good fuck.

Sie haben den ganzen Tag durchgefickt. They fucked all day long.

Eier *pl.* balls, testicles ['eggs']

Ich haue dir gleich eine in die Eier! *said as a warning* ['I'm about to punch you in the balls']

Du gehst mir auf die Eier! You're a pain in the ass! ['you're getting into my balls']

Fick, -(e)s, -e *m.* (act of) fucking

Unser Fick war prima! That was a great fuck we had!

ficken 1. to fuck 2. to stick in 3. to slide around

Er fickt sie. He's fucking her.

Sie ficken. They're fucking.

Fleck: Flecken ins Bettuch machen to have a wet dream,

have a nocturnal emission ['to make spots on the sheets']

Fotze, -, -n *f.* 1. cunt 2. bitch *term of abuse, said of a woman*

Frauenlob, -es *n.* prick, penis ['woman-praise']

Furz, -es, ̈e *m.* fart
  einen Furz lassen   to let a fart
  Du hast einen Furz im Hirn! You have some wierd ideas! ['you have a fart in the brain']
  Er macht einen Donnerschlag aus einem Furz. He's making a mountain out of a molehill. ['he's making a clap of thunder out of a fart']

furzen to fart
  Ich furze auf deine Hilfe. I don't give a shit about your help. ['I fart on your help']

Gummi, -s, -s *m.* rubber, condom

Gurke, -, -n *f.* dong, penis ['cucumber']

haben to lay, copulate with ['to have']
  Er hat sie gehabt. He made it with her.

herumfurzen to drive around (aimlessly) ['to fart around']

herunterholen to jack off, masturbate (to completion) ['to fetch down']
  Er hat sich einen im Scheißhaus heruntergeholt. He jacked off in the bathroom.

Holz breasts ['wood']
  Sie hat viel Holz vor der Tür. She's really stacked. ['she's got a lot of wood in front of the door']

Hosenscheißer, -s, - *m.* coward ['pants-shitter']

Hundertfünfundsiebziger, -s, - (175-er) *m.* fag, homosexual ['one hundred seventy-fiver']

Kacke, - *f.* crap, shit

kacken to shit, take a crap
  Ich muß kacken. I've got to take a crap.

Knollen *pl.* balls, testicles

Koffer: Du hast einen Koffer stehen lassen. You cut the cheese (i.e., you farted). ['you left a suitcase standing']

kommen *said of man or woman* to come, have orgasm
Mir kommt's bald. I'm about to come.
Ich komme! I'm coming!

Loch, -es, ̈er *n.* twat, vagina ['hole']

machen: Sie haben es gemacht. They went all the way (i.e., they copulated). ['they made it']

Möse, -, -n *f.* pussy, vagina

Muschi, -, -s *f.* pussy, vagina ['kitty cat']

Nüsse *pl.* nuts, testicles ['nuts']

Oberarsch, -es, ̈e *m.* shitass, bastard ['super-ass']

Pariser, -s, - *m.* condom ['Parisian']

Pfeife, -, -n *f.* dick, penis ['pipe, whistle']

Pflaume, -, -n *f.* pussy, vagina ['plum']

Piller, -s, -(s) *m.* dick, penis

Pillerman, -es, ̈er *m.* dick, penis

Pimmel, -s, -s *m.* peter, penis

pinkeln to pee, urinate

Piß, -es *var. of* Pisse

Pisse, - *f.* piss
Dieses Bier schmeckt wie Pisse. This beer tastes like piss.

pissen to piss
Ich pisse dir gleich ans Bein! You're cruisin' for a bruisin'! *said as a threat* ['I'd just as soon piss on your leg']

Pissoir, -s, -e *n.* urinal

Pißort, -s, -e *m.* urinal ['piss-place']

Puff, -s, -e/-s *m./n.* whorehouse

Puffmutter, -, ̈ *f.* madam (of a whorehouse) ['whore-house-mother']

Pussie, -, -s *f.* pussy, vagina

rammeln to screw, copulate with ['to buck, rut']

rummachen 1. to screw 2. to neck, pet

Sack, -es, ̈e *m.* balls (and scrotum) ['bag, sack']

   Du fauler Sack! You lazy bastard! ['you lazy scrotum']

   Du kannst mir mal an den Sack fassen! Go fuck yourself! ['you can just take hold of my balls']

Scheiß, -es *m.* shit, crap, junk

   Scheiß! Shit! *expresses anger, annoyance*

   Sie spielen einen Scheiß. What a piece of shit (music) they're playing.

   Scheiß machen to fuck up, bungle

Scheiß- *prefixed to words to give a negative connotation*

   Scheißprofessor no-good professor ['shit-professor']

   Scheißwetter fucking, no-good weather ['shit-weather']

   Mein Scheißauto ist kaputt. My fucking car is on the blink.

Scheißbolle, -, -n *f.* turd, piece of shit

Scheißdreck, -s *m.* 1. shit, junk 2. bullshit, nonsense ['shit-crap']

   Er redet immer Scheißdreck. He's always bullshitting.

   Sie hat viel Scheißdreck eingekauft. She bought a lot of shitty junk.

   Sie verkaufen viel Scheißdreck an die Turisten. They sell a lot of shitty junk to the tourists.

   So ein Scheißdreck! Goddammit!

   Das geht dich einen feuchten Scheißdreck an! That's none of your fucking business! ['that concerns you like wet shit']

Scheiße, - *f.* 1. shit 2. junk, crap 3. bullshit, nonsense

   Mach' keine Scheiße! Don't fuck up! ['don't make any shit']

Er steht bis zum Hals in der Scheiße. He's up shit creek (i.e., he's in trouble). ['he's standing in shit up to his neck']

(Verfluchte) Scheiße! Damn it! Shit!

den Betrieb wieder aus der Scheiße ziehen to patch up a mess ['to pull the deal back out of the shit']

Er hat ihn aus der Scheiße gezogen. He helped him out of a jam. ['he pulled him out of the shit']

scheißen, schiß, geschissen to shit

Ich scheiße ihn an. I don't give a shit about him. ['I shit on him']

Ich scheiße darauf. I don't give a shit about it. ['I shit on it']

Auf deine Hilfe scheiße ich! I don't give a shit about your help. ['I shit on your help']

Scheiß der Hund drauf! I don't give a fuck! ['may the dog shit on it']

Da scheißt der Hund ins Feuerzeug! Fuck a duck! *expresses surprise, disbelief, dismissal, rejection* ['then the dog shits on the cigarette lighter']

scheißegal indifferent ['shit-equal']

Das ist mir scheißegal. I don't give a flying fuck. ['to me that is equal to shit']

Scheißerei, - *f.* the trots, diarrhea

scheißfreundlich exaggeratedly friendly ['shit-friendly']

Scheißhaus, -es, ̈er *n.* bathroom, outhouse ['shit-house']

Ich muß auf's Scheißhaus gehen. I've got to go to the can.

Du langes Scheißhaus! You tall son of a bitch!

Scheißer, -s, - *m.* 1. coward 2. weak person 3. shit-ass, bastard ['shitter']

Scheißkerl, -s, -e *m.* shitass ['shit-guy']

Schickse, -, -n *f.* 1. whore 2. bitch *term of abuse*

Schiffe, - *f.* piss

schiffen 1. to take a leak, piss 2. to rain
Es schifft. It's raining.

Schiß, -es, -e *m.* 1. shit 2. fear
Er hat Schiß. He's scared shitless.

Schleimscheißer, -s, - *m.* 1. ass-kisser, sycophant 2. coward ['slime-shitter']

Schlitz, -es, -e *m.* crack, vagina ['slit, slot']

Schwabbelbusen, -s, - *m.* pendulous tits ['jelly-tits']

Schwanz, -es, ⁻e *m.* prick ['tail']
Leck mich doch am Schwanz! Suck my cock!

Schwanzgesicht, -(e)s, -er *n.* ugly face ['prick-face']

schwul *adj.* faggy, homosexual

Schwule, -n, -n *m.* fag, homosexual

Seich, -(e)s *m.* 1. piss 2. bullshit, nonsense 3. badtasting drink, swill

Seiche, - *f., var. of* Seich

seichen 1. to piss 2. to bullshit, talk nonsense

Seicherin, -, -nen *f.* bitch *term of abuse* ['woman who pisses']

Ständer, -s, - *m.* hard on, erection ['piller, post']
Er hat einen Ständer. He's got a hard on.

Stecher, -s, - *m.* stud, ladies' man ['stinger']
Ist das dein neuer Stecher? Is that the guy who's been servicing you lately?

steif *adj.* erect, erected (penis) ['stiff']
Er hat einen Steifen. He's got a hard on.

Strich: Sie geht auf den Strich. She walks the streets (i.e., she's a prostitute).

Strichmädchen, -s, - *n.* whore ['street girl']

Süsse, -n, -n *m.* fag, homosexual ['sweetie']

Titte, -, -n *f.* tit

Traum: einen feuchten Traum haben to have a wet dream, have a nocturnal emission

treiben: Er hat es mit ihr getrieben. He made it with her (i.e., had sex with her).

Tripper, -s, - *m.* clap, gonorrhea

verarschen to make an ass (out) of, fool

Vogel: Er hat einen toten Vogel in der Tasche. He let a fart. ['he's got a dead bird in his pocket']

vögeln to fuck

    Er wollte schon lange mit ihr vögeln. He's wanted to fuck her for a long time.

    Er vögelt mit ihr. He's fucking her.

    Sie vögelt mit ihm. She's fucking him.

    Sie haben die ganze Nacht gevögelt. They fucked all night.

Votze *var. of* Fotze

Voze *var. of* Fotze

warm *adj.* homosexual ['warm']

    warmer Bruder fag ['warm brother']

Warme, -n, -n *m.* fag, homosexual

wichsen 1. to beat off, masturbate 2. to fuck ['to wax, polish']

ziehen: Er hat einen ziehen lassen. He let one (i.e., he let a fart).

RUSSIAN

GUIDE TO RUSSIAN PRONUNCIATION

Vowels. Vowels with an acute accent (á, é, ó, ú, í, ý) are pronounced more energetically than unaccented vowels (a, ă, u, i, ў); in some cases they also have a qualitative difference:

á	*a* in f*a*ther (but closer to Spanish *a*)
a	like *á* but shorter, less forcefully pronounced
ă	*a* in *a*bout
é	*e* in b*e*t
ó	*o* in h*o*rse (*au* in t*au*t, but more rounded)
ú	*oo* in b*oo*t (but closer to French *ou* in f*ou*tre)
u	· same as *ú*, but pronounced less energetically
í	*i* in mach*i*ne (but closer to French *i* in mach*i*ne)
i	*i* in p*i*n
ý	*y* in s*y*lvan. A high central vowel; the tongue rises toward the center of the palate and the lips are unrounded (for *i* the tongue rises toward the front of the palate, for *u*, toward the back).
ў	same as *ý*, but pronounced less energetically

Consonants.

y	*y* in *y*oung
p	*p* in s*p*in
b	*b* in *b*ut
t	*t* in s*t*op
d	*d* in *d*og
f	*f* in *f*un
v	*v* in *v*ote
k	*k* in s*k*ull
g	*g* in *g*un
s	*s* in *s*ong
z	*z* in *z*one
l	*l* in si*l*ver
r	*r* in *r*un, but trilled
m	*m* in *m*op
n	*n* in *n*ote
h	*h* in *h*ot (closer to German *ch* in a*ch*)
ts	*ts* in ha*ts*
ch	*ch* in *ch*eeze
sh	*sh* in *sh*riek
sh'	*sh* in *sh*e; longer than *sh*, with the blade of the tongue closer to the palate
zh	*s* in plea*s*ure

Soft consonants. Most of the consonants may be either "hard" (unpalatalized) or "soft" (palatalized). In pronouncing the soft consonants the tongue moves upward toward the palate. This results in the impression of a weak "y" sound between the consonant and a following vowel. Soft *n'* is close to French *gn* in oi*gn*on; soft *l'* is close to Italian *gl* in co*gl*ione. Soft *t'* and *d'* have slight fricative (*s* and *z*, respectively) offglides. The difference between *k'*, *g'*, and *h'* and their hard counterparts is less noticeable to the American ear. Consonants followed by an apostrophe are soft. The following consonants have hard and soft forms:

p b t d f v k g s z l r m n h
p' b' t' d' f' v' k' g' s' z' l' r' m' n' h'

The consonants *sh, zh, ts* are always hard; *ch* and *sh'* are always soft.

Unless otherwise noted, the nominative and genitive singular of nouns and the imperfective infinitive and first and third persons singular of verbs are given.

барда́к -а́ (bardák) 1. whorehouse 2. mess, disorder

барда́чный (bardáchnўy) messy, confused ['pertaining to a whorehouse']

бардáчное де́ло (bardáchnăyă ďélă) mess, confusion

бздеть бзжу/бзджу бздит (bzďéť) 1. to fart (silently) 2. to bullshit 3. to pollute the air 4. to be frightened

Не бзди! (ni bzdí) Don't be a fucking coward!

бздун -а́ (bzdún) 1. person who farts frequently 2. coward

блядова́ть -ду́ю -ду́ет (blidaváť) 1. to whore 2. to carouse, dissipate

бля́дский (bľátskiy) 1. pertaining to a whore 2. goddamned

бля́дская рабо́та (bľátskăyă rabótă) hard/tedious work ['whore's work']

блядь -и (bľáť) 1. whore 2. bitch, slut 3. shitass, bastard

вы́ебать -ебу -ебет (výyibăť) *perf.* 1. to fuck 2. to punish 3. to chew out, scold 4. to pull out of a hat, obtain from nowhere

Он хо́чет её вы́ебать. (ón hóchit yiyó výyibăť) He wants to fuck her.

вы́пердок -дка (výpirdăk) brat, child *abusive* ['someone produced by farting']

говённый (gav'ónnўy) shitty

говно́ -á (gavnó) 1. shit 2. shitass, bastard 3. crap,
junk 4. bullshit, nonsense

Своё говно́ не воня́ет. (svayó gavnó ni van'áyit)
One's own shit doesn't stink.

Ло́жка говна́ в бо́чке мёда. (lóshkă gavná v bóchki
m'ódă) a fly in the ointment ['a spoonful of shit in
a barrel of honey']

конфе́тку сде́лать из говна́ (kanf'étku zd'ĕlăt' iz gavná) to make something of good quality out of poor
material ['to make a piece of candy out of shit']

Он с говна́ пе́нки снима́ет. (ón z gavná p'énki sn'i-
máyit) He's a greedy bastard. ['he skims the foam
off of shit']

болта́ться как говно́ в про́руби (baltáttsă kak gavnó
f prórubi) to be flighty, unstable ['to bob like shit
in a hole in the ice']

говню́к -á (gavn'úk) shitass, bastard

гондо́н -a (gandón) 1. rubber, condom 2. inept, weak
man

го́сти: К ней го́сти пришли́. (k n'éy gósti prishlí) *euph.*
She's on the rag. She's having her period. ['she has
guests']

дава́лка -и (daválkă) nympho, sexually promiscuous
woman ['woman who gives']

дриста́ть -ищу́ -и́щет (dristát') to have the runny shits,
have diarrhea

дристли́вый (dristlívўy) having runny shits

Одна́ коро́ва дристли́ва—всё ста́до передри́щет.
(adná karóva dristlívă, fs'ó stádă piridrísh'it) One
bad apple spoils the barrel. ['if one cow has the runny shits, the whole herd will come down with it']

дрочи́ла -ы (drachílă) masturbator [*from* дро-
чить]

дрочить -чу́ дро́чит (drachít') to jack off, masturbate
Ка́ждый дро́чит, как он хо́чет. (kázhdÿy dróchit kak ón hóchit) Different strokes for different folks. ['each person jacks off as he pleases']

Ду́нька Кулако́ва: Он игра́ет с Ду́нькой Кулако́вой. (ón igráyit z dún'kăy kulakóvăy) He's getting it from Madame Palm and her five daughters (i.e., he's masturbating.) ['he's playing with Dunya Kulakova'; a pun on 'Kulakova' (*from* кулак 'fist')]

еба́ло -а (yibálă) 1. mouth 2. face [*from* ебать 'to fuck']
Закро́й еба́ло! (zakróy yibálă) Shut your fucking mouth!

ёбаный (yóbănÿy) fucking, goddamned
Иди́ к ёбаной ма́тери! (idí k yóbănăy mátiri) You motherfucker! ['go to a fucked mother']

ёбарь -я (yóbăr') 1. stud, cunt-chaser 2. boyfriend, lover ['one who fucks']

еба́ть ебу́ ебёт *past tense* **ёб/еба́л ебла́/еба́ла ебли́/еба́ли** (yibát') 1. to fuck 2. to cuss out 3. to bitch at, find fault with 4. to fuck (over), treat unfairly
Он еба́л её ка́ждый день. (ón yibál yiyó kázhdÿy ďén') He fucked her every day.

еба́ть мозги́ (yibát' mazgí) to bug, pester ['to fuck the brains']

Ёб твою́ мать! (yóp tvayú mát') 1. Fuck off! 2. Goddamn it! 3. I'll be damned! 4. I don't give a fuck! ['(I) fucked your mother']

Я в рот его́ еба́л! (ya v rót yivó yibál) Fuck him! ['I fucked him in the mouth']

Э́то меня́ не ебёт! (étă min'á ni yib'ót) I don't give a fuck about it! ['it doesn't fuck me']

Хо́лод ебёт. (hólăt yib'ót) It's colder than a witch's

tit.   ['the cold is fucking']

еба́ться (yibáttsă)   1. to fuck   2. to screw around (with), tinker (with)

Они́ еба́лись всю ночь. (aní yibális' fs'u nóch) They fucked all night.

Она́ ебётся как ко́шка. (aná yib'otsă kak kóshkă) She fucks like a mink (very energetically).   ['she fucks like a cat']

Еби́сь она́ в рот! (yibís' aná v rót) She can go fuck herself! ['may she be fucked in the mouth']

ебли́вый (yiblívўy) liking to fuck

е́бля/ёбля (yébľă/yóbľă) 1. (act of) fucking   2. busy work, senseless activity

е́бля с пля́ской (yébľa s pľáskăy)   1. big party 2. noise, disorder   ['fucking and dancing']

жо́па -ы (zhópă)   1. ass, buttocks   2. ass-hole, anus 3. shitass, bastard

быть в глубо́кой жо́пе (býť v glubókăy zhópi) to be up shit creek, be in a fix ['to be in a deep ass-hole']

Брось ду́мать жо́пой! (brós' dúmăť zhópăy) Get your head out of your ass! ['quit thinking with your ass']

лиза́ть жо́пу (lizáť zhópu) to kiss ass, adulate ['to lick ass']

на чужо́й жо́пе в рай въе́хать (nă chuzhóy zhópi v ráy v'yéhăť) to sponge, take advantage of *smb.* ['to ride into paradise on someone else's ass']

приста́ть как ба́нный лист к жо́пе (pristáť kak bánnўy líst g-zhópi) to nag, pester ['to stick like a wet leaf to *smb's* ass']

Язы́к к жо́пе прили́п. (yizýk g-zhópi prilíp) The cat's got his (her, etc.) tongue. ['*his* tongue is stuck to *his* ass']

Иди́ в жо́пу! (idí v zhópu) Kiss my ass! ['go up *my* ass']

На ка́ждую хи́трую жо́пу есть хуй винто́м. (na kázhduyu hítruyu zhópu yesť húy vintóm) There's always someone smarter than you. ['for every smart ass-hole there's a prick (ready) to screw in']

Он без мы́ла в жо́пу ле́зет. (ón biz mýlă v zhópu ľézit) He's a real ass-kisser. ['he slides up one's ass without soap']

У него́ песо́к из жо́пы сы́пится. (u nivó pisók iz zhópў sýpitsă) He's getting senile. ['the sand is sprinkling out of his ass']

Ши́ре жо́пы не пёрднешь. (shýri zhópў ni p'órnish) Everyone has his limits. ['you can't let a fart bigger than your ass-hole']

жо́пник -а (zhópnik) 1. fag, homosexual 2. brown-nose, flatterer

жополи́з -а (zhăpalís) brownnose, flatterer

жо́почник -а (zhópăchnik) 1. fag, homosexual 2. ass-kisser, flatterer 3. ass-hole, bastard

заговня́ть -я́ю -я́ет (zăgavn'áť) *perf.* to fuck up, foul up [*from* говно́ 'shit']

заеба́ть -бу́ -бёт (zăyibáť) *perf.* 1. to wear out *smb.* by fucking 2. to fuck to death 3. to pester, exasperate
заеба́ть мозги́ *кому* (zăyibáť mazgí) 1. to fool 2. to brainwash ['to fuck *smb's* brains out']

залу́па -ы (zalúpă) 1. head of penis 2. foreskin 3. shit-ass
залу́па ко́нская (zalúpă kónskăyă) ass-hole, jerk ['horse's foreskin']
Пососи́ залу́пу! (păsasí zalúpu) Fuck no! *refusal to a request* ['suck a foreskin']

залупа́ться -а́юсь -а́ется (zălupáttsă) to be angry

Не залупа́йся! (ni zălupáysă) Don't get pissed off!

засе́ря -и (zas'ér'ă) *masc. & fem.* shitass ['one who has shit on himself']

засра́ть -сру́ -срёт (zasráť) *perf.* 1. to shit (on) 2. to dirty 3. to foul up

засра́ть мозги́ *кому* (zasráť mazgí) to fool, deceive ['to shit on *smb's* brains']

засра́ть глаза́ (zasráť glazá) to pull the wool over *smb's* eyes, deceive ['to shit in *smb's* eyes']

засра́ться -сру́сь -срётся (zasráttsă) *perf.* 1. to shit one's pants 2. to fuck up, bungle

Он засра́лся на экза́мене. (ón zasrálsă nă egzámini) He fucked up on the exam.

засса́ть -су́ -сы́т (zassáť) *perf.* to piss (on)

Он засса́л ему́ мозги́. (ón zassál yimú mazgí) He fooled the hell out of him. ['he pissed on his brains']

зассы́ха -и (zassýhă) *masc. & fem.* 1. person who pisses his pants 2. shitass, bastard 3. young girl *abusive*

ка́ка -и (kákă) *child language* doo-doo, shit

ка́кать -аю -ает (kákăť) to poop, defecate

конча́ть -а́ю -а́ет (kancháť) to come, have orgasm ['to finish']

ку́рва -ы (kúrvă) 1. whore 2. bitch, slut 3. shitass, bastard

малафья́ -й (mălaf'yá) come, semen

манда́ -ы́ (mandá) cunt, vagina

мандаво́шка -и (măndavóshkă) 1. crab, pubic louse 2. shitass, bastard ['cunt louse']

мине́т -а (min'ét) blow job, fellatio

Она́ сде́лала мне мине́т. (aná zďélălă mn'é min'ét) She gave me a blow job.

мине́тка -и (min'étkă) woman who gives blow jobs

мине́тчик -а (min'étchik) cunt-lapper, cunnilinctor

мудáк -á (mudák) fool [*from* мудé 'balls']

мудé -я́ *pl.* **мýди мудéй** (muďé) balls, testicles
Он дал емý по мудя́м. (ón dál yimú pă muďám) He kicked him in the balls.

мудéть -жý -ди́т (muďéť) to talk nonsense [*from* мудé]
Ну, не муди́! (nu ni mudí) Come on, don't bullshit!

муди́ться -жýсь -ди́тся (mudíttsă) to tinker with
Я цéлый день муди́лся с маши́ной! (ya tsélўy ďén' mudílsă s mashýnăy) I fucked around with that car all day!

набздéть (nabzďéť) *perf.* to let a big (silent) fart [*from* бздеть]

наебнýть -нý -нёт (năyibnúť) *perf.* 1. to cheat 2. to gorge, eat until stuffed
Он меня́ наёб на два рубля́. (ón min'á nayób na dvá rubľá) He screwed me out of two roubles.

накачáть -áю -áет (năkacháť) *perf.* to knock up, impregnate ['to pump up']
Он ей накачáл ребёнка. (ón yéy năkachál rib'ónkă) He knocked her up. ['he pumped up a child for her']

нáсморк: парúжский нáсморк (paríshskiy násmărk) clap, gonorrhea ['Parisian headcold']

насрáть -срý -срёт (nasráť) *perf.* to shit (on)
Мне на э́то дéло насрáть. (mn'é na étă ďélă nasráť) I don't give a shit about that. ['I could shit on that matter']
насрáть *кому* в кармáн (nasráť f karmán) to play a dirty trick on *smb.* ['to shit in *smb's* pocket']

насцáть -сцý -сци́т (nassáť) *perf.* to piss (on)

нахýйник -а (nahúynik) rubber, condom ['something which fits over the prick']

обосрáться -срýсь -срётся (abasráttsă) *perf.* 1. to shit on oneself 2. to fuck up, bungle 3. to be cowardly

Я обосра́лся на экза́мене. (yá abasrálsă nă egzámini)
I really fucked up on the exam.

обсца́ть -сцу́ -сци́т (abassát') *perf.* to piss (on)
Это ле́гче чем два па́льца обосца́ть. (étă ĺéhchi
chim dva pál'tsă abassát') That's easy as pie. ['that's
easier than pissing on two fingers']

опизден́е́лый (apizdin'élўy) 1. befuddled 2. crazy
3. pissed off, angry [*from* пизда 'cunt']

опизден́е́ть -е́ю -е́ет (apizdin'ét') *perf.* 1. to become
exhausted 2. to become confused, befuddled 3. to get
pissed off, angry

ослоёб -а (aslayór) ass-hole, incompetent person
['donkey-fucker']

отсо́с -а (at-sós) blow job, fellatio
сде́лать отсо́с *кому* (zd'élăt' at-sós) to give *smb.* a
blow job

отсоса́ть -су́ -сёт (at-sasát') to blow, perform fellatio
['to suck off']
Она́ ему́ отсоса́ла. (aná yimú at-sasálă) She blew
him. ['she sucked *it* off for him']

отхуя́чить -чу -чит (at-huyáchit') *perf.* to beat, thrash
Он его́ отхуя́чил. (ón yivó at-huyáchil) He beat the
shit out of him.

отъеба́ться (at'yibáttsă) *perf.* to get out, leave
Отъеби́сь от меня́! (at'yibís' ăt min'á) Get the fuck
away from me!

охуева́ть -ва́ю -ва́ет (ahuyivát') (*perf.* охуе́ть) 1. to
be puzzled 2. to be amazed 3. to go nuts/crazy 4. to be
impressed [*from* хуй 'prick']
Ты что, охуе́л? (tý shtó, ahuyél) Are you out of
your fucking mind?

охуева́ющий (ahuyiváyush'iy) terrific, wonderful, very
good

охуе́ние -я (ahuyén'yǎ) (act of) going crazy

Надое́ла мне э́та рабо́та до охуе́ния. (nădayélă mn'é étă rabótă dă ahuyén'yǎ) I'm fucking bored with this work.

па́лка -и (pálkă) orgasm ['rod, stick']

Он ей три па́лки ки́нул. (ón yéy tri pálki kínul) He got it off with her three times. ['he tossed her three sticks']

пе́дрик -а (p'édrik) fag, homosexual

перде́ть -жу́ -ди́т (pirď'éť') 1. to fart 2. to bullshit

пёрднуть -ну -нет (p'órnuť') *perf.* to fart

Сказа́л, как в лу́жу пёрднул. (skazál kak v lúzhu p'órnul) He really put his foot in his mouth. ['he said it as if he'd farted into a puddle']

перду́н -а́ (pirdún) 1. person who farts frequently 2. weak, old man

перду́нья -и (pirdún'yǎ) woman who farts frequently

пердя́чий пар: Он идёт пердя́чим па́ром. (ón iď'ót pirď'áchim párăm) He's getting there on his own steam (i.e., on foot). ['he's going there (propelled) by fart steam']

перееба́ться -бу́сь -бётся (piriyibáttsă) *perf.* to fuck (many or all)

Она́ перееблась со всем го́родом. (aná piriyiblás' sa fs'ém górădăm) She's fucked everyone in town.

пи́дор -а (pídăr) 1. fag, homosexual 2. shitass, bastard

пизда́ -ы́ (pizdá) 1. cunt 2. bitch, woman *abusive* 3. *said of a man* shitass, bastard

Он дал ему́ по пизде́ меша́лкой. (ón dál yimú pă pizď'é mishálkăy) He really raked his ass over the coals (i.e., told him off). ['he hit him on the cunt with a spatula']

Моя́ пое́здка в Москву́ пиздо́й накры́лась. (mayá

payéstkă v maskvú pizdóy nakrýlăs') My trip to Moscow fell through. ['my trip to Moscow was covered by a cunt']

Она́ торгу́ет пиздо́й. (aná targúyit pizdóy) She's a a whore. ['she deals in cunt']

Это ну́жно, как пизде́ буди́льник. (étă núzhnă kăk pizd'é budíl'nik) That's as worthless as tits on a boar hog. ['I (you, etc.) need that like a cunt needs an alarm clock']

Она́ даёт пизду́. (aná dayót pizdú) She puts out, she fucks. ['she gives cunt']

Ты что, с пизды́ сорва́лся? (tý shtó, s pizdý sarvál-să) Where the fuck have you been all your life? *said to someone who appears ignorant* ['did you just pop out of a cunt?']

Иди́ в пизду́! (idí f pizdú) Go fuck yourself! ['go up a cunt']

Пизда́ тебя́ роди́ла! (pizdá tib'á radílă) You fucking bastard! ['a cunt gave birth to you']

пиздану́ть -ну́ -нёт (pizdanút') *perf.* 1. to slug, hit 2. to swipe, steal

пиздёж -а́ (pizd'ósh) bullshit, nonsense

пизде́ть -зжу́ -зди́т (pizd'ét') 1. to bitch, complain 2. to chatter 3. to bullshit

Не пизди́! (ni pizdí) Don't bullshit me!

пи́здить -зжу -здит (pízdit') (*perf.* спи́здить) to swipe, steal

пиздобра́тия -и (pizdabrátiyă) group of buddies, friends *usually derogatory* ['cunt-brotherhood']

пиздова́тый (pizdavátỹy) dense, stupid

пиздосо́с -а (pizdasós) shitass, bastard ['cunt-sucker']

пиздострада́тель -я (pizdăstradátil') horny, frustrated man ['cunt-sufferer']

пиздю́к -а́ (pizďúk) shitass, bastard

пиздюле́й: Он наве́сил ему́ пиздюле́й. (ón nav'ésil yimú pizďuľéy) He beat the fucking shit out of him.

пиздя́чить -чу -чит (pizďáchiť) to beat up, thrash

пипи́ (pipí) *child language* pee, urine

сде́лать пипи́ (zďélať pipí) to wee-wee, urinate

пи́сать -аю -ает (písăť) 1. to piss 2. to be hot for, be sexually attracted to

писто́н: Он ей поста́вил писто́н. (ón yéy pastávil pistón) He put it to her (i.e., copulated with her). ['he put the piston to her']

побляду́шка -и (păblidúshkă) 1. slut, unscrupulous woman 2. an easy lay/make, woman easily seduced [*from* блядь 'whore']

подма́хивать -аю -ает (padmáhivăť) 1. to wiggle the buttocks while having sexual intercourse 2. to submit to sexual intercourse

Тебя́ не ебу́т, ты не подма́хивай! (tib'á ni yibút, tý ni padmáhivăy) Mind your own fucking business! ['you're not being fucked, so don't wiggle your ass']

подъёбывать -аю -ает (paďyóbўvăť) 1. to make cutting remarks 2.to fuck skillfully (adapting one's movements to one's partner) [*from* ебать 'to fuck']

посра́ть -сру́ -срёт (pasráť) *perf.* to (take a) shit

посца́ть -сцу́ -сци́т (passáť) *perf.* to (take a) piss

приеба́ться -бу́сь -бётся (priyibáttsă) *perf.* to bother, pester

Что ты приеба́лся ко мне? (shtó tý priyibálsă ka mn'é) What the fuck are you bugging me for?

ра́ком: еба́ться ра́ком (yibáttsă rákăm) to fuck "dog style" ['to fuck like a crab']

сблядова́ться -ду́юсь -ду́ется (zblidaváttsă) *perf.* 1. to become a whore 2. to become dissolute

сика -и (síkă) 1. pussy, vagina 2. girl who wets her pants

сикать -аю -ает (síkăť) *child language* to pee, urinate

сикель -я (síkiľ) clit, clitoris

скурвиться -влюсь -вится (skúrvittsă) 1. to become a a whore 2. to become depraved 3. to betray, inform on [*from* курва 'whore']

спиздить -зжу -здит (spízdiť) *perf.* to swipe, steal
Кто спиздил его книгу? (któ spízdil yivó knígu) Who the fuck stole his book?

срака -и (srákă) ass-hole, anus
Били его и в рот, и в сраку. (bíli yivó i v rót, i f sráku) They kicked his ass from hell to breakfast. ['they hit him in the mouth and in the ass']

срать сру срёт (*less common:* серю/серу серет, *3. pl.* серют/серут) (sráť) 1. to shit 2. to fart

ссака *var. of* сцака

ссаки *var. of* сцаки

ссать *var. of* сцать

стоять: У него стоит. (u nivó stayít) He's got a hard on/erection ['his is standing']

суходрочка -и (suhadróchkă) busy work, senseless activity ['dry masturbation']

сцака -и (ssákă) piss, urine

сцаки (ssáki) piss, urine

сцать сцу сцит, *3. pl.* сцат/сцут (ssáť) to piss, urinate
Сцать я на него хотел. (ssáť ya nă nivó haťél) Piss on him! To hell with him! ['I would piss on him']

сцаться сцусь сцится *3. pl.* сцятся/сцутся (ssáttsă) to piss one's pants

тётка: Тётка пришла. (ťótkă prishlá) (Her) period has begun. ['her aunt has arrived']

титька -и (tíťkă) tit

трамва́й: Она́ попа́ла под трамва́й. (aná papálă păt tramváy) She got gang-banged/gang-raped. ['she fell under a streetcar']

уёбывать -аю -ает (uyóbўvăť) to leave, get out
Уёбывай! (uyóbўvăy) Get the fuck out!

усёр -а (us'ór) (act of) shitting
Я смея́лся до усёру. (yá smiyálsă dă us'óru) I laughed till I shit my pants.
Он еба́л её до усёру. (ón yibál yiyó dă us'óru) He fucked the shit out of her.

усра́ться усру́сь усрётся (usráttsă) *perf.* 1. to shit one's pants 2. to fuck up, be unsuccessful
Он усра́лся на экза́мене. (ón usrálsă nă egzámini) He fucked up on the exam.
Усра́ться мо́жно! (usráttsă mózhnă) Fuck! That's incredible! ['one could shit one's pants']

хе́зать -аю -ает (h'ézăť) to shit

хер -а (h'ér) dick, penis *synonymous with* хуй *in various expressions*

хуева́тый (huyivátўy) mediocre, undistinguished [*from* хуй 'prick']

хуёвина -ы (huyóvină) 1. bullshit, nonsense 2. crap, worthless thing 3. thing, small object

хуёвый (huyóvўy) lousy, wretched, worthless
—Как пожива́ешь? —Хуёво! (kák păzhўváyish? huyóvă!) —How are you? —Fucking lousy!

хуесо́с -а (huyisós) cocksucker, shitass ['cock-sucker']

хуй ху́я (húy) prick, penis
хуй моржо́вый (húy marzhóvўy) shitass ['walrus prick']
хуй на колёсах (húy nă kaľósăx) shitass ['prick on wheels']
Он ни хуя́ не зна́ет! (ón ni huyá ni znáyit) He

doesn't know a fucking thing!

Емý одúн хуй, кто ты есть! (yimú adín húy któ tý yésť) He doesn't give a fuck who you are!

Хуй егó знáет! (húy yivó znáyit) How the fuck should I know!

Хуй с ним! (húy s ním) Fuck him!

Он до хуя́ баб переебáл. (ón dǎ huyá báp piriyibál) He's fucked a hell of a lot of women.

Идú нá хуй! (idí ná-huy) Go fuck yourself! ['go to a prick']

Пососú хуй! (pǎsasí húy) I wouldn't give you the sweat off my balls! ['suck a prick']

Я хуй на негó положúл. (yá húy nǎ nivó pǎlazhýl) I don't give a flying fuck about him. ['I put a prick on him']

На хуя́ э́то мне нýжно? (nǎ huyá étǎ mn'é núzhnǎ) What the fuck do I need that for?

Уéду нá хуй. (uyédu ná-huy) I'm getting the fuck out of here for good.

с гýлькин хуй (z gúľkin húy) 1. very tiny 2. very small amount ['about the size of a pigeon's prick']

Ты что, с хýя сорвáлся? (tý shtó, s húyǎ sarválsǎ) Where the fuck have you been all your life? (i.e., don't you know anything?) ['did you pop off of a prick?']

Хýем грýши околáчиваю. (húyim grúshў akaláchivǎyu) I'm not doing a fucking thing. ['I'm whacking down pears with my prick']

и рýбку съесть, и нá хуй сесть. (i rýpku s'yésť i ná-huy s'ésť) to eat one's cake and have it too ['to eat the fish and sit on the prick']

на чужóм хуýю в рай въéхать (nǎ chuzhóm huyú v ráy v'yéhǎť) to sponge, take advantage of *smb.* ['to ride into paradise on someone else's prick']

хуйня -й (ḣuyn'á) 1. bullshit, nonsense 2. crap, junk

хуярить -рю -рит (ḣuyáriť) 1. to beat, thrash 2. to cover (a certain distance)

цéлка -и (tsélkă) 1. cherry, hymen 2. virgin 3. pretentious woman

Он ей сломáл цéлку. (ón yéy slamál tsélku) He broke her cherry.

цéлочка -и (tsélăchkă) cherry, hymen

Он раскололся как цéлочка. (ón răskalólsă kak tsélăchkă) He cracked (i.e., broke down under interrogation). ['he cracked like a hymen']

я́йца яйц (yáytsă) balls, testicles

Егó схватили за я́йца. (yivó s-hvatíli za yáytsă) They've got him by the balls.

Иди слонý я́йца качáть! (idí slanú yáytsă kacháť) Get the fuck out of here! ['go swing an elephant's balls']

Не крути мне я́йца! (ni krutí mn'é yáytsă) Don't try to bullshit me! ['don't twist my balls']

COMMON AMERICAN ENGLISH
OBSCENITIES

Stylistically neutral and euphemistic forms (when given) follow the taboo words and are separated by a semicolon.

adulate, to to brown-nose, suck ass, kiss ass, kiss up to

anal intercourse ass-fuck, butt-fuck

angry, to be/become to be/get pissed (off), be peed off; to be teed off, be ticked off, fly off the handle

annoy, to to gripe smb's ass/balls, be on smb's ass, bug (smb's ass)

annoyance pain in the ass, pisser

anus ass, ass-hole (arse-hole), butt, butt-hole, bung hole

bad, low quality shitty, crappy, cruddy, fucked

blunder fuck up, screw up, snafu; boner

blunder/fail, to to fuck up, screw up; to foul up, mess up, goof up, blow it

blunderer fuck-up, screw-up

bore, to to bore smb's ass off; to bore smb. stiff

break wind, to to fart, let/lay a fart, let one, cut the cheese

breasts tits, boobs (bubs), boobies (bubbies), knockers, pair

brothel whorehouse, cat house, call house

buttocks ass (arse), butt, buns, gee-gee (gigi), can, tail, prat(t); bottom, rump, rear(end), seat

care about, to to give a (flying) fuck about, give a shit about, give a damn about

chatter/gossip/boast, to to shoot the shit/crap/bull, shovel the shit

complain, to to bitch, piss (and moan)

completely, thoroughly from hell to breakfast

condom rubber, Trojan, skin, scumbag; prophylactic

copulate (with), to to fuck, screw, lay, ball, bang, bump, hump, ride, have, make, give it to, stick/put it to, make it with, go to bed with, sleep with, make love (to), have sex with

copulate quickly, to to wham-bam, bunny fuck, tear off a piece of ass, have a quickie

copulate, to persuade to to get into smb's pants/jeans/drawers, score, make out

copulation from behind dog style, dog fashion

courage balls, guts

coward candy ass; chicken, yellow-belly

cunnilinctor cunt-lapper, cunt-licker

cunnilingus eating out, French, French style/way

cunnilingus, to perform to eat (out), suck, lick

defecate, to to shit, crap, take a shit/crap, dump a load, squat; to go, poo-poo, grunt, do "number two"

diarrhea the runny shits, the runs, the trots, the G.I.'s, the G.I. shits, Montezuma's revenge

difficult task/job ball buster, ball breaker, ball wracker

egotist hot shit, shit on wheels

ejaculate, to to come, get one's rocks off, get one's load off, get one's nuts off, get one's gun off, shoot one's load/wad, drop/shoot one's cookies, shoot off, drop one's load, get it off, cream

erection hard on, bone-on, boner, hard

erection, to get/have an to get/have a hard on, get it

on/up, have lead in one's pencil

exhausted   fucked out; pooped

expletives   fuck (it)! shit! piss (on it)! fuck a duck! horse shit! (god)dammit! (god)damn! oh, fuck! I'll be fucked!

fail, to cause to   to screw/fuck smb. up

falsehood   shit, crock (of shit), crap, piece/pile of shit

falsehood, to tell a   to shit, bullshit, shovel the shit

feces   shit, crap, turd; doo-doo, poo(-poo), poop, hocky

fellate   to blow, suck (off), give smb. head, eat, French

fellatio   blow job, head (job), French (style sex)

fellator   cock sucker

fix, to be in a   to be up shit creek (without a paddle), get/have one's ass in a sling; to be in hot water, be in a mess

flirt   prick-tease, cock teaser

fool   ass-hole, shit-head, dipshit, douche bag

frightened   scared shitless, pucker-assed

gang rape   gang bang

general terms of abuse   **male** mother fucker, fucker, shitass, ass-hole, cock sucker, dipshit, shit, turd, shit-head, pile of shit, prick, horse's ass, piss-ant, son of a bitch, bastard   **female** cunt, bitch, slut, whore

hell! go to   fuck you! fuck off! go fuck yourself! screw you! up your ass! up yours! stick it (up your ass)! cram it! shove it! suck my cock! eat me! kiss my ass!; drop dead! buzz off! get lost! go fly a kite!

homosexual   cock sucker, fag, faggot, queer, fairy, pansy, swish, queen, homo

hymen   cherry; maidenhead

ignorant, to be   not to know (jack) shit, not to know shit from Shinola, not to know one's ass from a hole in the ground

impregnate   to knock up, give smb. a big belly

intensifiers fucking, mother-fucking, cock-sucking, frigging, goddamned

lecher cocksman, cunt-chaser, stud; skirt-chaser

lecherous on the make, on the prowl

leave hurriedly, to to haul ass, bag ass, shag ass

loaf, to to fuck off/around, screw off/around, jerk off, fart around

lust for, to to have the hots for (smb's body), be hot for

masturbate, to to jack off, beat off, jerk off, beat one's meat, flog/beat the dummy, flog one's dong, pound one's pud, whack off, play with oneself

menstruate, to to be on the rag, have the rag on; to have one's period/monthly

misinformed full of shit/crap, full of bull(shit)

much, many out the ass, up the ass, up the ying-yang

nonsense shit, bull(shit), crap

penis prick, cock, pecker, dick, tool, meat, dong, peter, gun, rod, pole, weenie

penis, having a large well-hung, hung, hung like a bull

pet, to to feel up, feel, fingerfuck, dry fuck/hump

pregnant, to be to be knocked up, have a big belly

prostitute whore, hooker, ass peddler, streetwalker

prostitute, to be a to whore, peddle one's ass, hustle, hook, walk the streets

prostitute's client john, trick

prostitutes, to pursue to go whoring, be a whoremonger/whore-hopper

pubic hair bush, short hair

reprimand, to to chew/cuss smb's ass (out), ride smb's ass

ruin, to to fuck up, screw up; to foul up, mess up

sad, to be to drag (one's) ass

sanitary napkin rag

semen come (cum), jizm (jissom), jizz, cream

senseless activity fucking around, screwing around

sexual intercourse (an instance of) fuck, screw, piece (of ass), roll (in the hay), action

sexual intercourse, group daisy chain

sexually aroused, to be to be horny, be hot (to trot), have hot pants, be on the make

sycophant kiss ass, suck ass, ass-kisser, ass-sucker, brown-nose, brownie

testicles balls, nuts, rocks, family jewels

thrash, to to beat the shit/hell out of, beat the fuck out of, kick smb's ass

tinker with, to to screw/fuck/fart around with

toilet shitter, crapper, shit-house, can, head, john, pot; potty, W.C., lavatory

toilet paper ass-wipe, ass-wiper, tail timber

trash, worthless object shit, crap, piece of shit/crap, pile of shit; junk

treat unfairly, to to fuck (over), fuck (over) royally, screw (over), stick/put it to, shaft, piss on

unfortunate shit out of luck, fucked (up)

urinate, to to piss, take a piss, take a leak/whiz, pee; to wee-wee, wet, tinkle, relieve oneself

urine piss, pee; wee-wee

vagina cunt, pussy, box, snatch, twat, meat, slit, clit, crack

venereal disease clap (clapp), syph (siff), crud

woman (or vulva) as object of cunnilingus eatin' stuff, table grade, hair pie, box lunch

woman as sexual object (piece of) ass/tail/meat, piece, poontang, make, hump, lay, twat

work hard, to to bust (one's) ass, bust one's balls

yes you bet your ass! fucking-A!

ABBREVIATIONS

adj.	adjective
dim.	diminutive
euph.	euphemism
f./fem.	feminine (noun)
fig.	figurative
hum.	humorous
jm.	jemandem
m./masc.	masculine (noun)
n.	neuter (noun)
perf.	perfective
pl.	plural
qc.	qualcuno
q.c.	qualche cosa
qn.	quelqu'un
smb.	somebody
smth.	something
var.	variant

Scythian Books
P. O. Box 3034
Oakland, California 94609